She's Alone

Sasha Joy

Contents

She's Alone

Chapter 1

The Assignment

Elena was used to the gritty underbelly of New Jersey. As a journalist for the Trenton Gazette, she thrived on stories that blended fact and intrigue, and lately, nothing captivated her more than the string of murders in New Orleans' French Quarter. Whispers of a vampire-like killer had drawn her in, and she was determined to uncover the truth.

Boarding a plane, Elena felt a mix of excitement and dread. New Orleans was a city steeped in much mystery, its shadows heavy with tales of the supernatural, but as she touched down, the humid air of New Orleans enveloped her, and she knew she was in for a wild ride. Gathering her luggage and checking into the hotel, Elena pulled her long black hair into a ponytail as she straightened her skirt, checking her makeup in a small, hallway mirror of the hotel, she could see her fragile brown eyes were slightly exhausted from the trip.

After settling into her suite, Elena decided to shower and sleep for the remainder of the night. Tomorrow would begin her journey, her investigation in search of any answers about the vampire-style serial killer.

Chapter 2

The Quarter's Shadows

The French Quarter was very much alive with various music and faint laughter, yet beneath the mere surface lay an unsettling tension. The locals spoke in hushed tones about a dark figure that only stalked the night, an evil creature who lured victims with charm before vanishing them into the darkness. Elena felt the pull of the supernatural, both thrilling and terrifying. As she ventured through the cobblestone streets of the Quarter, asking many questions about the murders, she wasn't getting very far. The locals only spoke of myths and legends.

As the night sky darkened, Elena was about to call it a day and return to her hotel, when, at that moment, she turned the corner of Royal Street, she saw a tall man, dark and mysterious. He was looking straight at her with a cigarette in his hand.

After she explored the winding streets all day within the French Quarter, she finally encountered Julian, a captivating stranger with piercing, hollow eyes that seemed to see straight through her. He was enigmatic, charming, and utterly magnetic. His mere eyes were hypnotizing, with their dark blue hues sparkling under the moonlight. His dark hair was long and neatly pulled back, showing the masculine structure of his jaws.

He spoke with a deep, French accent. Their mere connection seemed instantaneous, a dangerous dance of flirtation that ignited a spark within her that she hadn't felt in many years.

After a quaint introduction, Elena suggested for Julian to accompany her to the little cafe that was just beyond Bourbon Street...

Chapter 3

The Seduction

After Elena ordered a small coffee and a doughnut, she asked Julian many questions about his experience within the Quarter. Julian shared faint tales of the French Quarter, weaving a web of local folklore with a slight edge of truth, yet each story seemed to hint at a deeper darkness lurking just beyond the vibrant facade. She was beginning to think that Julian was much like the locals that she had spoken with earlier, only telling small legends and dark myths about the place.

Elena still found herself entranced in his stories, not just his tales, but by Julian himself. He was different, charming, almost too perfect in his nature, much too alluring. That's when she excused herself from their conversations by telling him it was awfully late, and she headed to her hotel in a rush.

The next evening, Elena searched the whole day for Julian, but he was nowhere to found. As the sun fell behind the old buildings of the French Quarter, she finally saw him. He was standing under the flickering gas lights of Jackson Square. As she approached him, Julian leaned in and whispered false secrets into her ear, that sent shivers down her spine.

Elena was confused, but she was also drawn to him, caught in a hypnotic trance, it seemed.

He spoke of immortality and eternal love, themes that played against her rational mind, but there was just something in his hollow gaze that hinted at much danger.

Feeling overwhelmed, though she never spoke a word, she closed her eyes, as if she allowed him in. At that moment, she opened her eyes to find that Julian was gone... nowhere to be found. Elena was dumbfounded. She wasn't sure what just happened. Confused, embarrassed, she ventured back to hotel. She had to think on these few encounters with this mysteries, tall man called Julien.

Chapter 4

The Truth Revealed

As the murders escalated over the next few nights, Elena's investigation deepened. The police were unsettled, yet not really concerned. Their mere responses were, 'It's all under investigation, but no leads have been found.'

As she searched further into the alleyways where the victims were found, she discovered a mere pattern, a series of evidence from the victims that linked them all by a darker thread... a club that catered to those who sought the mere thrill of the darkness within the night. It was a simple business card just resting on the cobblestone street of the alley of the last victim's belongings.

Her research had led her to the realization that these individuals were obviously partying at this dark, vampire-style club at the end of Royal Street. As she stood at the entrance of the creepy, hidden club, Elena glanced again at the business card. That was when she noticed the owner's name... Julian. Her heart raced with this newfound revelation. 'Could all these supernatural tales be true?'

Now she was torn between her journalistic instincts and her growing inner, lustful feelings for Julian. 'What if he was connected to these murders? What if he was the actual killer, the actual predator?'

Elena stepped inside.

Confronting him in a candle-lit room, as he dwelled alone at a corner table, she demanded the truth. Elena wanted to know who he was exactly. Julian's smile was faint, as his fangs glistened in the pale light of the club, and with a deep, soulful gaze, he revealed his true nature. He confessed to Elena that he was centuries old, cursed to walk the night, and yet he had never met anyone like her.

Elena caught herself 'believing' his words, yet she knew it had to be impossible.

Chapter 5

The Struggle

Caught in an overwhelming whirlwind of mere emotions, Elena struggled to reconcile these lustful feelings deep within her, every time she encountered Julien, she felt so vulnerable. Her hidden feelings for Julian were slowly trying to surface, yet she could sense the horrifying truth, she knew deep inside that this mysteries, hypnotizing man, or vampire, was the killer.

Elena was determined to expose him though, to end his reign of terror within the Quarter, but each encounter with him seemed to leave her more conflicted.

Julian would distract her by making 'promises' to her of a life beyond the mundane, a mere world where she could escape the inevitability of death itself. His hypnotizing eyes would seem to convince her into believing that he wanted her for eternity, and Elena eventually started to believe him.

After many nights of meeting Julian at the club, Elena was captivated, completely forgetting her reasoning. Their mere relationship spiraled into a very dangerous game of lust and passion. Julian seduced her with mere visions of a joyous life unbound by time, while she faintly fought to keep her heart and her morals intact, but with each stolen, lustful kiss, she felt her mere resolve weakening.

Chapter 6

The Climax

The night of the final confrontation had arrived. Weeks had passed and Elena was merely focused on being in Julian's cold embrace, yet she knew he was evil, dangerous. She knew deep within that it had to come to an end. Julian was a killer, an undead creature who fed on mortal women, drinking their blood out of greediness, leaving them in the alleyways.

Armed with the mere knowledge that she had gathered in evidence, mere devices that were supposed to take down a 'vampire'; Elena was determined to end this fantasy. She lured Julian to the back of the club, into the back alley, where the darkness overshadowed them.

It was there, among the mere echoes of faint laughter and distant music, that she revealed her true intentions to him, but Julian sensing her betrayal, transformed into a fearsome creature of the night. His fangs showed fiercely under the moonlight, as he made his attack.

A fierce struggle ensued, a mere battle of wills and strong desires. Elena fought not just for her mere life, but for the lives of those he had brutally taken.

In a moment of dark clarity, she plunged a silver dagger, an old relic she had discovered during her research, straight into his heart. Julian fell to the dampened ground. Elena quickly knelt beside him, as he faded into his eternal death, she kissed his frozen lips one last time...

Chapter 7

The Aftermath

As Julian slowly crumbled to mere dust, Elena felt a void within her. The myth of Julian being a 'vampire' was really a reality. It was true.

She had succeeded in catching the killer and uncovering the hidden secrets to all the murders, but it was at a great cost, a major price to be paid.

In Julian's final moments, as Elena and him struggled, battled, Julian had bitten her on her neck. This little bite had sealed Elena's fate, unaware at the time, as Elena kissed Julian on his frozen lips and said, "It's finally over", her lips brushed against the blood that rested on his lips. As his mere eternal blood stained her mouth, she was now immortal.

The pain ran through her entire body as she passed out.

After awakening, Elena realized she still in the alley, alone. She quickly regained her composure and returned to the hotel.

Elena was now truly alone, slightly afraid at what she was becoming, she was the one who was cursed now with this cruel immortality, and the mere knowledge that she could never truly escape it. She would, now, be the one hidden in the shadows, preying on mortals for their blood.

Several nights passed, Elena finally succumbed to her blood hunger, yet she did not kill anyone, she merely got her blood fill and erased their mere memory of her. It was quite easy... she did not have to harm another human being to survive. After many trials and errors, Elena eventually accepted what she had become.

Not returning to her home in New Jersey, Elena arranged for her belongings to be moved here in the French Quarter, in an apartment on the backside of Royal Street. She took over the ownership of Julian's club and let go of her old life.

Elena did turn her story of Julian into the newspaper back in New Jersey, by mailing it in, after she quit her journalist job. She penned the story with a heavy heart, it was a sad tale of lust, love, and loss, of mere seduction and betrayal, of a city that would forever haunt those who dwell within it forever. The headline of her story in the Trenton Gazette in New Jersey read as follows... 'The Vampire of the French Quarter, A Love Story Turned Deadly'.

Although, the murders by Julian were never solved, Elena knew she had found her answers...

Epilogue

Alone in the Night

As Elena walked the now familiar streets of the French Quarter, she felt the weight of her eternity pressing down on her.

Elena was no longer just a mere journalist, she was now a keeper of a dark secret, a wanderer of the night, a mere creature of the darkness, caught between the two worlds, the living and the undead.

Each night, as the moon casts its silver glow, she would find herself staring into the mere darkness, knowing she was now forever alone, left to roam the streets of the French Quarter through all eternity. As she journeyed into her unknown eternal damnation, she felt that she was no longer a journalist, but a simple myth, a creature of the night...

The End.

She's Alone

By: Sasha Joy